LIONEL
MESSI

A Little Golden Book® Biography

For Christopher, my favorite soccer buddy —R.L.

By Roberta Ludlow

Illustrated by Nomar Perez

A GOLDEN BOOK • NEW YORK

rhcbooks.com
Educators and librarians, for a variety of teaching tools, visit us at RHTeachersLibrarians.com
Library of Congress Control Number: 2023930103
ISBN 978-0-593-65217-6 (trade) — ISBN 978-0-593-65218-3 (ebook)
Printed in the United States of America
10 9 8 7 6 5 4 3 2 1

Lionel Andrés Messi was born on June 24, 1987, in Rosario, Argentina. His parents, Jorge Messi and Celia Cuccittini, called him Leo.

Leo fell in love with soccer—which is called football in most countries—when he was very young. He played all the time with his older brothers and cousins.

When Leo was four years old, he joined a local youth team. His father was the coach, but his grandmother Celia was his biggest fan. She went to all his training sessions and games.

Sadly, she died before his eleventh birthday. Ever since then, whenever Leo scores a goal, he celebrates by looking up and pointing toward the sky in tribute to his grandmother.

Leo was asked to join the youth system of Newell's Old Boys, one of the biggest teams in Rosario, when he was eight. He became their star player and scored more than 230 goals!

The kids on the youth team would often perform ball tricks during halftime at the professional games. They would balance the ball on one foot, juggle the ball with both feet, and back heel the ball over their heads! Leo's skills entertained the fans and caught the attention of coaches for the best teams in South America and Europe.

Leo was always smaller than his teammates. Doctors prescribed medicine that could help him grow, but it was very expensive, and Leo's parents couldn't afford it.

The world-famous soccer club FC Barcelona offered to pay his medical bills if he joined their youth team. So thirteen-year-old Leo and his family packed up and moved to Spain.

He was often homesick living in a new country, but Leo was always happy when he was playing soccer.

Just a few years later, Leo went from the youth league to La Liga—Spain's top professional soccer division. At seventeen years old, he became the youngest player and goal scorer in La Liga history! And this was only the beginning. Leo would go on to set many more records with FC Barcelona.

In 2009, FC Barcelona won the Champions League, the Spanish Super Cup, and the La Liga title. That same year, Leo won his first FIFA World Player of the Year honor, called the Ballon d'Or award.

Lionel Messi has had many nicknames through the years. His family called him Leo. Childhood friends called him the Flea because he was so small. Sports reporters in Spain called him the Atomic Flea because he was small *and* super fast. But most people know him by the name on the back of his jersey: MESSI!

Messi can make a perfect pass.

He can dribble through defenders.

And he can SCORE!

Goooooal

Messi has won more trophies and has set more records than any other soccer player! He scored the most goals for one team, he has the longest scoring streak in La Liga, and he has won six European Golden Boot awards and eight Ballon d'Or trophies—just to name a few.

And the biggest prize
was yet to come!

Even though Messi lived and played in Spain, he still had a strong connection to the country where he was born. So when it came time to decide which national team to play for, he chose Argentina.

He played on Argentina's 2005 FIFA World Youth Championship squad, represented the country in the 2006 FIFA World Cup, and helped them win the gold medal at the 2008 Olympic Games.

Messi was named captain of Argentina's team in 2011. In 2014, under his leadership, they made it to the World Cup final for the first time in twenty-four years!

And in 2022, at the age of thirty-five, Messi led Argentina to win the ultimate prize: the FIFA World Cup!

Messi's family is always there to cheer him on. In 2017, Messi married Antonela Roccuzzo. They first met more than twenty years earlier, when Messi played on the same youth team as Antonela's cousin. The fancy wedding took place in their hometown of Rosario.

The couple has three sons, Mateo, Thiago, and Ciro.

Messi's contract with FC Barcelona expired in 2021. He was sad to leave the team he had been with for so many years.

Messi agreed to play for Paris Saint-Germain. With a new team came a new home—Messi moved from Spain to France.

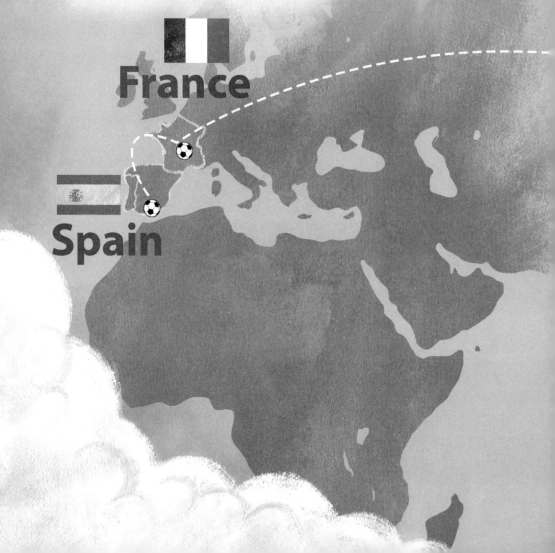

Just two years later, he was on the move
again—this time to the United States.
Playing for Inter Miami in Florida brought
Messi closer to his home and family in Argentina.

Off the soccer field, Messi has been involved with many charities for children. As a UNICEF Goodwill Ambassador, he traveled to Haiti after an earthquake left many kids and their families without homes, food, or clean water.

He also started the Leo Messi Foundation. Inspired by the medical expenses he had as a child, it helps give children from low-income families access to healthcare, schools, and sports.

Always working hard to be the best he can be at a sport he loves has earned Messi another nickname. People call him GOAT because he's the Greatest of All Time!